the calligrapher's work book

JIM BILLINGSLEY

When you feel confident endorse this page
with name and details.

Photography: David Sinclair
Editing: Pamela Newland

ISBN 0 947338 30 6

Axiom
Adelaide
South Australia

preface

This **Calligrapher's Work Book** has been compiled in answer to the most re-occuring questions asked by students of calligraphy. It caters for the very beginning scribe to the calligrapher who has reached a standard in their work where they may wish to experiment a little further or even undertake some commissioned work.

Language is international and so is writing — and the same problems can occur whatever the language you are writing. Suitable for classroom use or individual study, this book will provoke a need to try something different; be it with your fast developing 'individual' script or a new form of laying out your work .

Learn how to sit, and what the writing hand (whether right or left) is doing. Learn how to gain confidence with your calligraphy and have a bit of fun at the same time. You'll find that by practice and perseverance you will be able to enthuse others — no matter what age they are.

No particular emphasis has been placed on the type of pen you should use — and there are many commercially available — but rather more on the shapes that you should make when writing with the implement of your choice. The proof of this statement rests with the reader: find and cut a quill yourself, and amazingly, the idiosyncrasies of your writing are reflected on the page by feather.

The author and publisher felt the need for a straightforward work book on calligraphy—based on knowledge gained by teaching the subject.

The work of Martin Billingsley an ancestor of the author who invented the copybook form of writing. Written in 1618 with a quill pen on vellum it was the beginning of *acceptable handwriting* for everyone. He taught Charles 1 to write when Charles was the Prince of Wales and Martin was a scribe at the Bodleian College Library, Oxford.

A a.a.a.a.b.b.b.b.c.c.c.c.d.d.d.d.e.è.e.e.f.f.f.f.ff.g.g.g.~
g.g.gh.h.h.h.h.i.i.i.i.ÿ.k.k.k.k.l.ll.ll.l.m.m.m.m.n.~
n.n.n.n.o.o.oo.o.p.p.p.p.g.g.g.:g.r.z.r.r.s.st.t.fs.
t.t.t.tt.tt.v.v.v.u.u.u.w.w.w.v.x.x.x.y.yo.y.z.z.&

A.B.C.D.E.F.G.H.I.K.L.M.
N.O.P.Q.R.S.T.V.W.X.Y.Z

CONTENTS

introduction

In the Royal Observatory, at Greenwich in London is a simple solid silver cube known as the *Inch*. This is the cube that every inch was measured from.
But ...
nobody has *stored* away in a retrieval system the letter 'A', so there is no perfect model to go by, nor an exact reproduction of any particular script. We copy from the basis that was devised by scribes many years ago, and there has been much improvisation along the way.

So, here in this work book, and to be shared by others, is *my* very personal interpretation of the Italic, Gothic and Uncial Scripts. Like me, and given time to practice, you will devise your own personal variations on a theme that has been set.

There are few rules, except do not expect to become a calligrapher overnight — it doesn't happen that way. Do relax with the subject — it is possible to *shut off* in a crowded class-room.

Have fun *making your mark*. If you enjoy this experience, let the publisher know and we will venture further together into the exciting world of calligraphy...

Jim Billingsley

posture

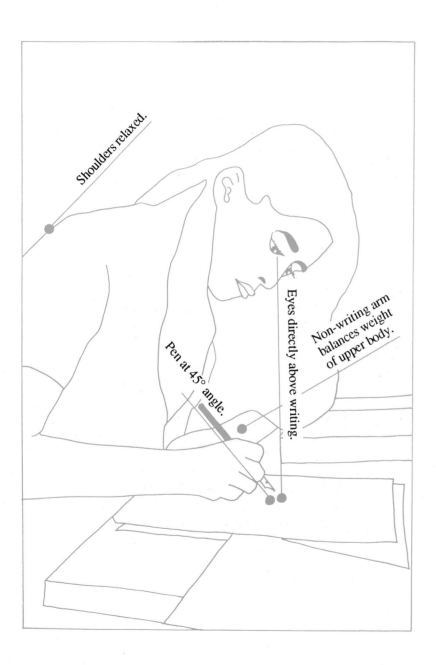

Shoulders relaxed.

Eyes directly above writing.

Non-writing arm balances weight of upper body.

Pen at 45° angle.

Posture is critical if you are to write neatly and for long periods. Try writing on a sloping surface, but remember to keep the work directly ahead of both eyes and not to one side. Use a pad of paper — blotting, if you can get it — under the writing hand. This will stop perspiration, natural oils and acids from your skin getting onto the writing surface.

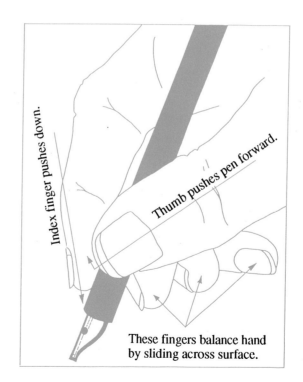

Index finger pushes down.

Thumb pushes pen forward.

These fingers balance hand by sliding across surface.

~an adventure~ in self~esteem for all ages...

1 Be *comfortable* and at *peace* when you are writing.
2 Write something that you *want* to write.
3 Ensure that you have a box of tissues nearby — *just in case.*
4 Find some pleasant and relaxing music.
5 *Don't hurry* into it. Try to pre-plan each line and check the depth of the line spacing between lines.
6 If the telephone rings, let it continue until you can answer.
7 Spelling may suffer at first.
8 You might not be doing your BEST calligraphy TODAY; TOMORROW it will be BETTER!

In order to start, and assuming that you are sitting correctly, we must now attempt some very basic but extremely important exercises. The zigzag pattern allows the pen to function thinly on the *up* strokes, and thick on the *down* strokes. (The angle is *exactly* 45° when this happens effectively).

The 'C' pattern now allows the pen to travel in a circular motion, when maintaining the 45° angle.

The other shapes are basic shapes made by the pen when attempting the Italic script. Practice at least a page of these using standard lined paper.

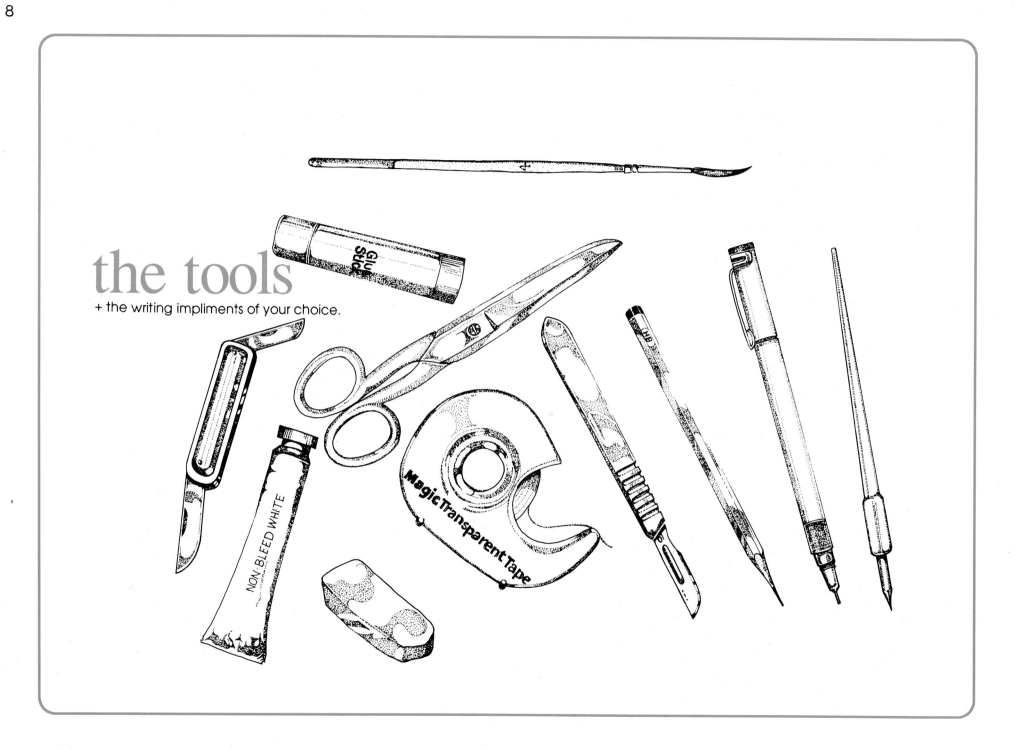

the tools

+ the writing impliments of your choice.

1 Study the letterforms for a long time before putting pen to paper. You will then know which of them will be likely to bother you.

2 Begin with the Italic script, — a more natural hand for most persons to come to grips with.

3 *Always* use a standard lined pad to practice, and when you are competent, move up to a good quality practice paper and a ruled grid sheet to suit the pen width. (You will find a series of grid sheets towards the back of this work book).

4 Don't write for the sake of writing. You will find that you really have to be *in the mood* sometimes.

5 So, after the basic exercises, practiced earlier, let's begin...

the 'Italian' script

The Italic or *Italian* Writing Script.

This rhythmic, flowing script came to us from the Papal Chancery many centuries ago. It was chosen as a 'book script' because it was easier to do than the Gothic letterforms and therefore, *much* faster. It developed through the great writing masters of Italy, and later to the whole of Europe, as the basis for our handwriting today. The script lends itself to our natural handwriting angles and can be flourished in quite a spectacular way without ruining legibility. It is a *social* form of writing and I believe, the hardest to learn.

a b c d e e e f f

g g h h h i j k k l

m m n n n o o p Q r

s s s t u v w x y z

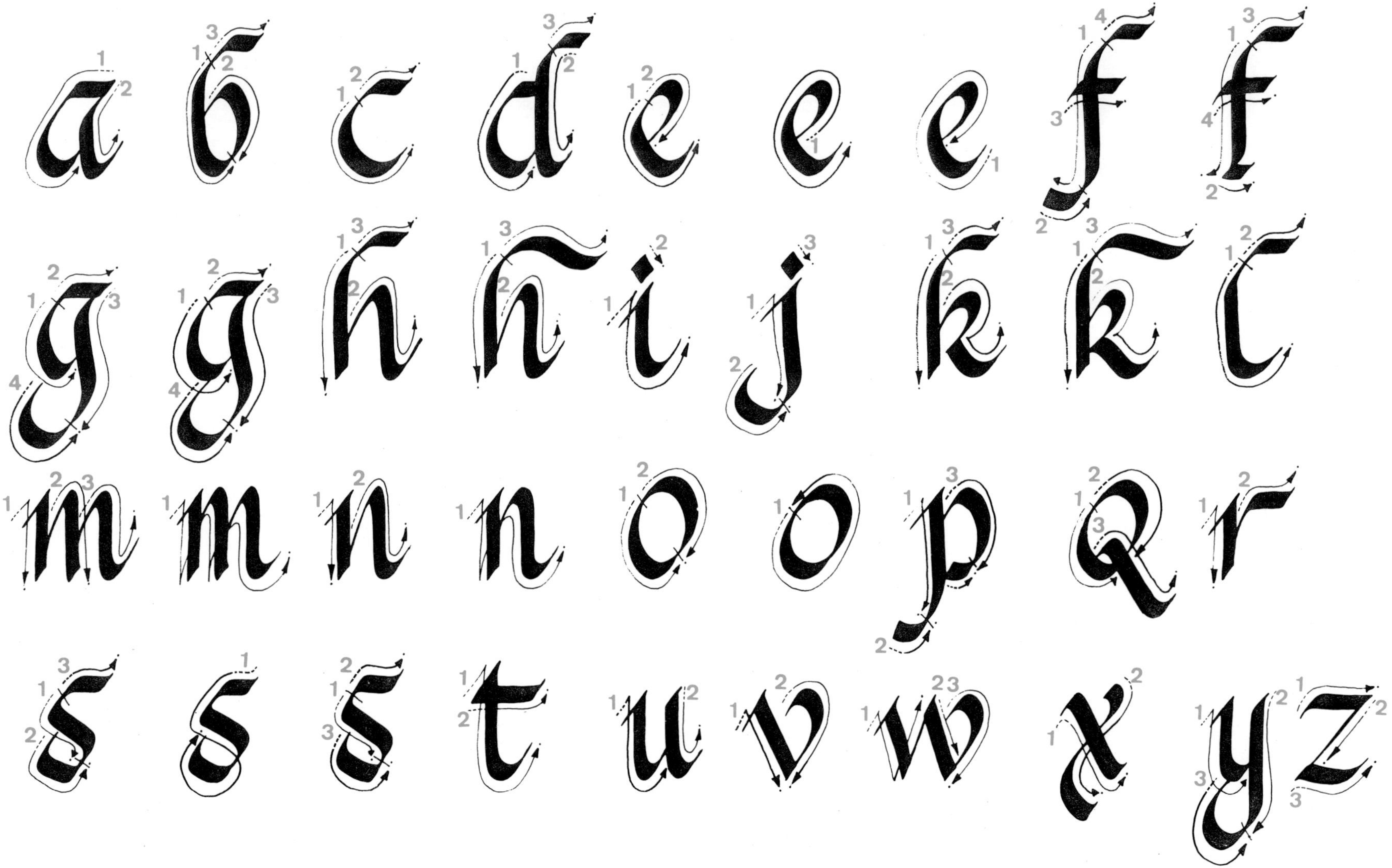

On lined paper, the capitals or *majuscule* letters should be two lines high. This will bring them close to the proportion of the smaller or *minuscule* letters.

the Gothic script

GOTHIC.
The most beautiful script ever devised and
written. Sometimes called 'Olde English'
(wrongly) or Blackletter, it is an economical
way of setting many words on a page. You
can condense it (squash it up) or expand it,
but you cannot slope it. Remember that in
olden days this was the writing of the law or
the church, and that readers were in no great
hurry to read it as they would be today. I once
lettered the hymn sheets for a wedding in this
script, only to be told later that it took too long
to read to be able to sing it, so the organist
played alone!
ENJOY GOTHIC.

a b c d e f g h i
j k l m n o p q r
s t u v w x y z

THE 'SECRET' OF GOTHIC

Have you practiced the little *trick* with your downstrokes? If you have, and it is easier for you, try your first word <u>in Gothic</u>. Write *Rumpelstiltskin* as shown in the first example and then repeat it with some gentle flourishes. Do notice how the word now begins to *flow*. <u>But don't make it too curly!</u>

If it all seems too hard the first time that you try this script, *leave it alone*; put it away and read a book or something and try again tomorrow. I believe that you have to be in the mood to attempt this script.

Once you have mastered it, don't fall into the trap of writing *everything* in Gothic; I have had students who really can't write any other way, even though they were proficient at other scripts as beginners. Use Gothic sparingly, wisely and authoritatively. After all, it *is* the writing of the law and gets noticed — always!

minimum

cæsar scribet sciences

minimum aluminium

Impossible Words.
There are many hundreds of words that when
written in English, will not *scan* as you can see
from the examples above.

a b c d e f g h i j k l m n o p q r
s t u v w x y z

a b c d e f g h i j k l m n o p q r
s t u v w x y z

A B C D E F G H I J K L M N O P Q R
S T U V W X Y Z

AN EASIER FORM OF GOTHIC CAPITALS

monograms

These can be fun, but avoid Mc or O' at all costs! Triple initials are also difficult. When you are competent, it is a great way to show off your calligraphic creative prowess — especially on a black board.

Left-handers, or 'Sinister' writers, should bear in mind that some of the greatest scribes in history were left-handed. Only five or six letters are formed differently for the left hand, and it won't take you long to find these out.

left-handers

The left-hander has always been taught to see writing in reverse, as if learning in a mirror. Today, this is no longer the method used, as there are pens made especially for the left-handed writer. The right-hander pulls the pen across the page from left to right with the writing hand well in advance of the wet ink. To achieve this, the left-hander must push the pen in the same direction without smearing the previously written line; this can be remedied by holding the pen above or below the line of writing. Only extreme cases should attempt to write with the hand above the line — AND A RIGHT-HANDED NIB. In my experience, a proficient left-hander, after much practice and adjustment, will go on to conquer great and challenging horizons in writing.

It may help if the left-handed writer crouches over the work more in order to see the writing that the hand is doing. With patience and practice many of the problems will be overcome.

the Uncial script

UNCIAL — meaning 'one inch high' — was the script that was developed from the Roman and Greek letters that were in use in the sixth to eighth centuries. In Rome the Scribes were laboriously writing in Roman with their chisels, while other parts of Europe adopted the simple Uncial script. It is believed that this script style came to us from Scandinavia and was used by the conquering Vikings who took it with them into Scotland. 'Uncial' finally rested on an island between Scotland and Ireland where the monks used the script, and with great illuminated adornment, turned it into the basis of the Gaelic and later Anglo-Saxon tongues that we speak today.

A A B C D E F G H
I J K L M N O P Q
R S T U V W X Y Z

Find a short poem of your own choice and
write it out firstly on lined paper, and then
copy or even trace your work onto a better
quality paper; you will find Uncial Script a joy
to work with. There are no special angles or
rules, except that you do not slope it or look
for little letters. *What you see is what it is...*

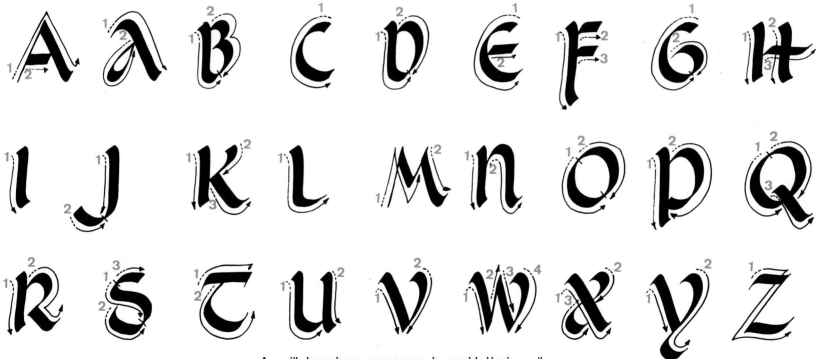

A quill, bamboo canepen, broad lettering nib or your widest calligraphy nib will do justice to the simple letterforms as you see them. The addition of writing Uncial in coloured inks adds to the charm of this delightful writing. 'Uncial' is also a social script, and can be used for poems, invitations, book texts or certificates — it also looks good for posters.

smudges

making mistakes...

Smudges usually happen when you are reaching to dip the pen, the phone rings or the pussy-cat is pacing and jumps up onto your work.

Depending upon the type of paper that you are using, you may be able to gently scrape away the problem with a sharp scalpel or razor blade. You *may*, when it is dry, be able to rub most of it away with an ink rubber. If this does not work, you have a retouching job on your hands. Using non-bleed white paint, available from all good art suppliers, and a fine brush, *retouch* by dabbing with the brush — do not overwet it — and if using a tinted paper, use water colour to tint the non-bleed white paint. Try this out on a corner of the work for colour matching.

THIER THEIR THEIR

The knack of *'overwriting'* is tricky, because you need to develop *blind spots* to enable you not to be able to *see* the previous writing. As with retouching, use a dabbing motion of the brush and paint away the unwanted strokes after you have overwritten. As you have gathered, if it doesn't work — Sorry — start again.

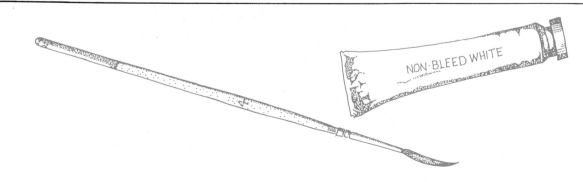

You should rehearse a piece of writing on ruled paper, ensuring that it is a) spelt correctly, b) spaced correctly, c) looks good overall.

'weight' of letters

abcde   abcde

abcde   abcde

abcde   abcde

abcde   abcde

abcde   abcde

Learn the weight and balance of your writing. Spindly letters are harder to form than weightier ones. Spindly letters, unless written very well, will look immature and ruin what may otherwise be a sensitive workpiece.

The clock of Life
The clock of Life
The clock of Life
The clock of Life
The clock of Life
The clock of Life

Which line looks and feels right?

This is to
COMEMORATE

The completion of the
FIRST PHASE
of the Development of the
new premises for the
HEART GROUP

————————————— —————————————
Secretary   President

This is to
COMMEMORATE

This trick is from the mind of experience. I have done it many times and never been detected! If the wokpiece is to go under glass you are very lucky. If not, use a good glue or gum (art cement is the best) so that it does not come adrift later. Ensure that the certificate is not rolled.

Using every piece of your ingenuity, correct the spelling error on another piece of *exactly* the same paper or board. Make sure that the colour and density of the ink or paint is identical to the wrongly spelt word on the workpiece. Cut out as a panel. Outline the panel in colour or gold paint, painting right up to the edge including the edges of the paper of the panel and mount it down with art cement. Say a tiny prayer. Leave overnight.

Try not to smile when you present it to the recipient.

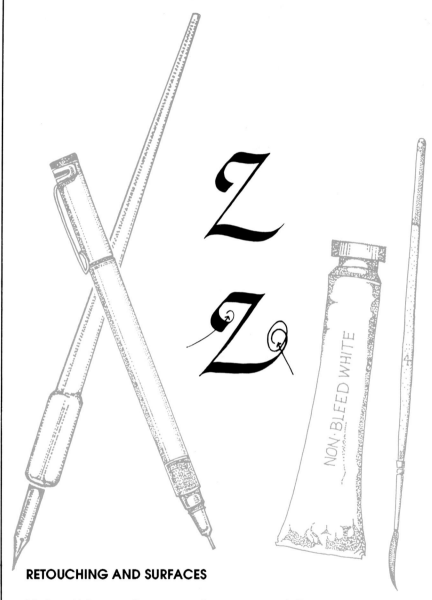

RETOUCHING AND SURFACES

<u>Hint</u>:   Using a fine mapping pen and the same ink as the main writing, retouch the 'fines' and 'serifs' if required.   Alternatively, use a very fine fibre or nylon tipped pen. Never dash into a piece of calligraphy without doing a paper test. — See page 30 for inks and paper.

repetitive, boring work

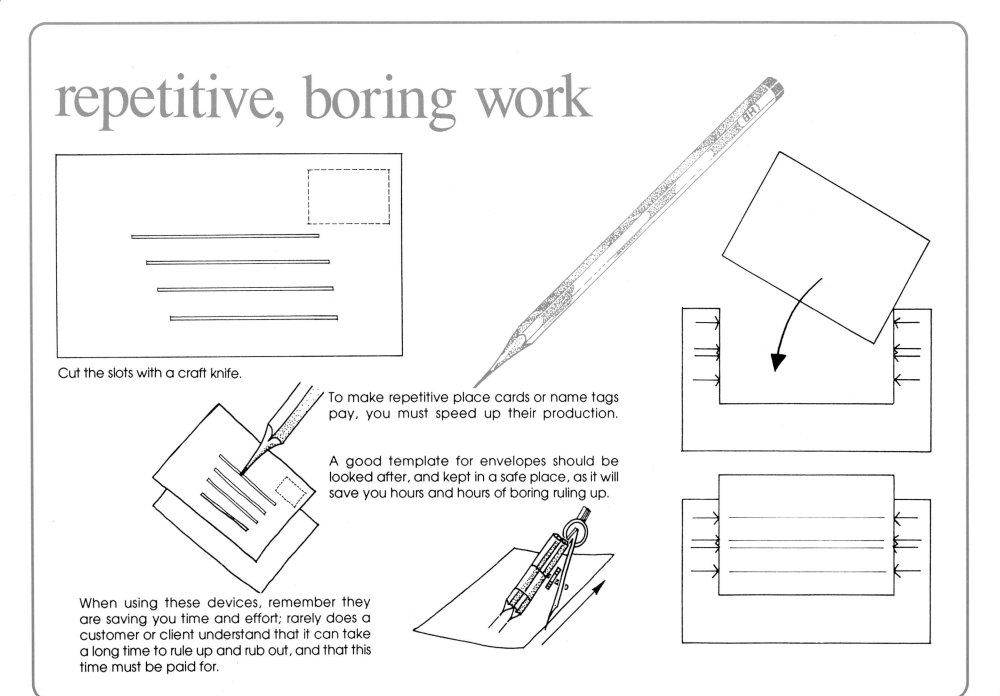

Cut the slots with a craft knife.

To make repetitive place cards or name tags pay, you must speed up their production.

A good template for envelopes should be looked after, and kept in a safe place, as it will save you hours and hours of boring ruling up.

When using these devices, remember they are saving you time and effort; rarely does a customer or client understand that it can take a long time to rule up and rub out, and that this time must be paid for.

How does a calligrapher handle tedious repetitive work?

It's quite simple really. INVOLVE OTHERS. Remember, *you* are the scribe and it's the ruling up and rubbing out that sometimes takes more time than the writing itself.

Just get organised — something like the diagram — and you will be able to amaze your helpers and let them feel part of the scheme of things.

GENERAL TIPS: If you make continual mistakes, just simply take a break for five minutes. Go for a walk; change your focal distance for a minute, then return to the project relaxed and ready to start again.

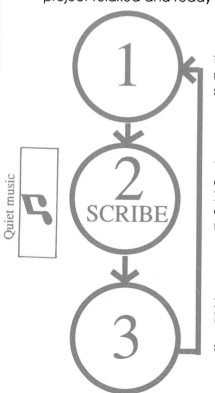

Quiet music

Using a template, 1 prepares items for the scribe. You will need a clean, silent worker for this task...

You — the scribe — must concentrate on spelling, spacing etc. Request silence when writing — except for the music — and you won't make mistakes...

3 checks spelling etc., rubs out guidelines, stuffs envelopes, hands back to 1 to rule up envelopes ready for scribe.

Some are small, neat, and a nuisance to both the post office and the calligrapher.

envelopes

Kinder to the reader and calligrapher and has room for stamps.

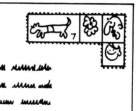

AIRMAIL

Remember to leave plenty of room for stamps, especially if the envelope is to go overseas, and remember the whims of the Post Office when it comes to commemorative stamp issues that *may* overlap your beautifully hand-lettered effort. Always leave room for airmail stickers.

Always use waterproof ink or fixative...

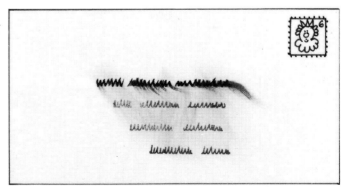

centreing lines

Don't guess the centre of the line of lettering. This simple and foolproof system works beautifully every time because it is a *mechanical* way of centreing. A badly centred piece of work looks shabby — even beautiful calligraphy, wrongly spaced and badly centred will be noticed as 'not quite right' by the reader.

1

Mary had a little lamb
its fleas were white
as snow,

And everywhere
that Mary went
the lamb
was sure to go.

Write the lines on lined paper, do not pay attention to centreing or spacing, but ensure the spelling is correct...

2

Mary had a little lamb
its fleas were white
as snow,

And everywhere
that Mary went
the lamb
was sure to go.

Fold each line you have written in half to find the centre and mark the fold...

3

Mary had a little lamb
its fleas were white
as snow,

And everywhere
that Mary went
the lamb
was sure to go.

Your paper should now look like this...

4

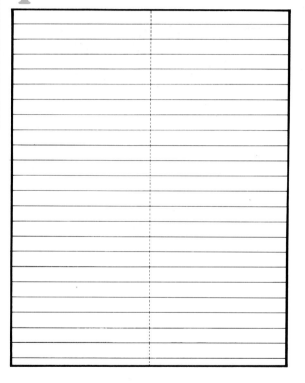

5

> Mary had a little lamb
> its fleas were white
> as snow.
>
> And everywhere
> that Mary went
> the lamb
> was sure to go.

6

> Mary had a little lamb
> its fleas were white
> as snow,
>
> And everywhere
> that Mary went
> the Lamb
> was sure to go.

Centreing Lines

Next, take a second piece of ruled paper, fold and mark centre...

Align centres of lines previously written with centre line of sheet and trace off...

Adjust the 'depth' of the work as well as the centreing when tracing. Use a lightbox for unruled papers.

inks & paper

1 Does the paper carry ink well?
2 Is the ink black or dense?
3 Will it dry?
4 Will the pencil lines rub out?
5 Will I be happy on this paper?

Inks vary to an enormous degree; *Indian ink,* for example, is jet black on most surfaces but ruins a commercial calligraphy pen. So, this ink should only be used for dip pens.

When you turn the cap of your ink bottle, does it have a gritty feel? If so, it is on the way out and should be discarded. Many blockages of pens are caused by stale ink.

An example of the same ink in the same pen written on different surfaces.

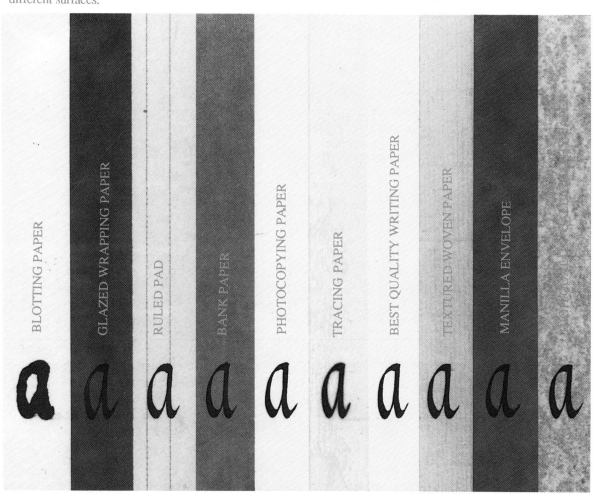

BLOTTING PAPER

GLAZED WRAPPING PAPER

RULED PAD

BANK PAPER

PHOTOCOPYING PAPER

TRACING PAPER

BEST QUALITY WRITING PAPER

TEXTURED WOVEN PAPER

MANILLA ENVELOPE

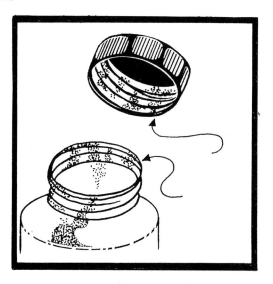

GOOD RELIABLE INKS ARE AVAILABLE FROM GOOD STATIONERS, but remember that all inks will react differently on different surfaces.

COMMERCIAL CARTRIDGE PENS

Pens do cease to flow occasionally. *Do not shake the pen.* The ink in a pen travels through a series of fine capillaries and vents rather like the carburettor in an engine. Shaking the pen will cause too much ink to flow and result in blots everywhere. That is, if the pen has not run out of ink!

ALL PENS

Simply wash your pens out in clean water from time to time; this ensures that the channels or reservoirs that carry the ink are clear, and that atmospheric dust and minute particles of dust — even from the writing surfaces are removed.

& nibs

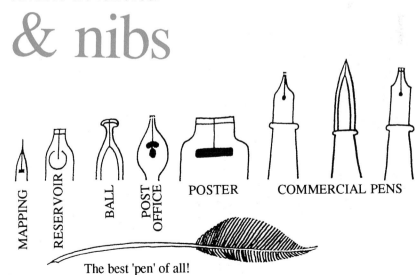

MAPPING RESERVOIR BALL POST OFFICE POSTER COMMERCIAL PENS

The best 'pen' of all!

flourishing

The clock of Life
is wound
but once

The clock of Life
is wound
but once

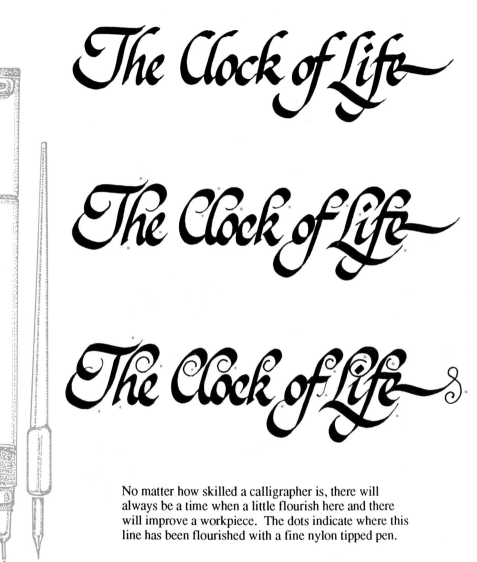

The Clock of Life

The Clock of Life

The Clock of Life

No matter how skilled a calligrapher is, there will always be a time when a little flourish here and there will improve a workpiece. The dots indicate where this line has been flourished with a fine nylon tipped pen.

INK
in the wrong places

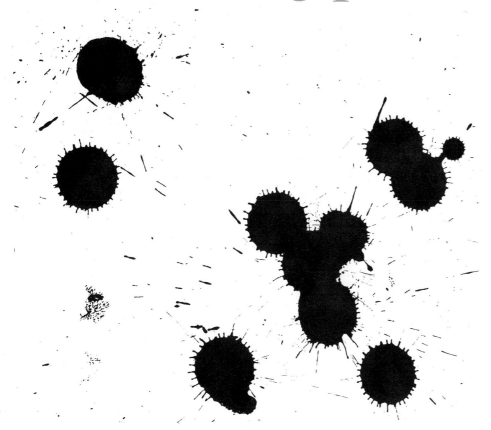

~alas, there is mych devilmynt in my ynk

INK ON CLOTHES OR FABRIC
1 Soak garment in *cold* water before the ink dries.
2 Gently rub stain until the ink disappears and spreads out.
3 Re-rinse in cold water several times before washing normally. (Do not use soap or detergent immediately as this will fix the ink forever).
4 If stain is stubborn soak overnight in a little bleach solution, (I suggest a weak mixture).

Ink varies; a good ink will stain beautifully, that's its job. Textiles also vary. <u>GOLDEN RULE</u>: don't do your calligraphy wearing your good clothes.

INK ON A WOODEN SURFACE
1 Mop spill but do not allow to dry completely.
2 Bleach applied with a cotton bud directly to the ink; this will erase it in seconds, and the area should then be sponged with lukewarm water.

INK ON YOU
How off-putting to shake a calligrapher's hand that is every colour of an ink-makers chart.
1 Catch ink stains while still wet, by rinsing in cold water. Most of the ink will wash away.
2 Scrub hands in lukewarm water and soap.
3 If ink has got underneath your fingernails, make up a solution of bleach and cold water, and soak hands for a few seconds. Used sparingly and sensibly, bleach is a powerful solvent for *all* inks...

INK ON CARPET
 A dreadful dilemma. Solution depends on a textile or wool carpet and the type of ink, etc. etc...
Don't write near good carpets or fabrics.

Southwell High   7 The Avenue
Anytown
51736

You are invited to attend a
Re-union of past students
at the Assembly Hall on
Tuesday 9th April at 6:30 pm

The presentation of Prizes will
take place at 7:30 pm followed by
Speeches.

Refreshments & Autographs

Signed

R.S.V.P MONDAY 2nd APRIL: 278 9313

Southwell High   7 The Avenue
Anytown
51736

You are invited to attend a
Re-union of past students
at the Assembly Hall on
Tuesday 9th April at 6:30 pm

The presentation of Prizes will
take place at 7:30 pm followed by
Speeches.

Refreshments & Autographs

R.S.V.P. MONDAY 2nd APRIL: 278 9313

Write on lined paper, spell correctly, check that you have <u>all</u> wording...

Fold a piece of paper to show where creases are, do not let photocopied or printed lines fall across a crease...

The final job.

The finished invitation will look like this — note that the front cover appears in position on the <u>back</u> of the sheet.

Mistakes are often made when addressing or writing. Keep in mind a further quantity of both invitations and envelopes may be required — I suggest a further 10%.

an invitation
Southwell High

which format?

Somebody has asked you to do their wedding invitations and you'd like them to be a little unusual...
There are dozens of different *formats* to choose from.

Experiment with formats *before* doing the writing.

Don't be frightened to give a pen a good wash. There will always be atmospheric dust and tiny chunks of ink behind the nib. Use rain or distilled water. Blot dry on an old tea towel.

pen care

Stoning a nib can bring it back to its original form. Use an oilstone — but no oil — and write in figure eights using your usual pressure but with water. Rinse nib as above. Do not over stone or you will cut stencils of your writing!

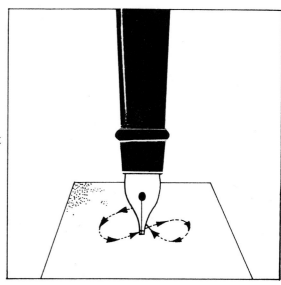

writing for reproduction

Rarely, if ever, is calligraphy reproduced the actual size that it is written. A reduction however slight, will clean-up the balance, weight and general look of a piece. Printers are always aware of the 'thicks and thins' of calligraphic workpieces, and excessive reductions of the image are for them a nightmare.

Writing for reproduction e.g. wedding invitations. When your writing is too light in weight it will lose its 'thins'. Whereas, writing that is too 'chunky' will fill-up and look disastrous.

It is always a good idea to reduce the image to the size required, by using a photocopier to gain some idea of how it will look when reduced by the printer.

Beware of printing calligraphy in gold ink; often it will look green and unattractive, and unless the printer is a specialist, do not expect any greater attention to the treatment of your work.

Too fine, will lose detail upon reduction.

Just right, will reduce nicely.

Too broad, will thicken up more upon reduction.

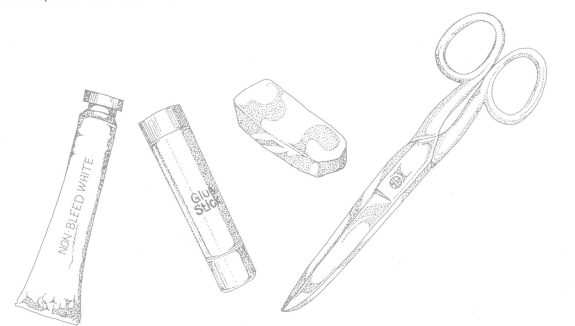

TRICKY SURFACES AND INKS

Problem:— Writing on a previously printed colour surface.

Solution:— Test if possible. If experiencing a run-back of ink, use a touch of egg white mixed with the ink. Try again, but allow longer time for drying.
<u>Do not blot.</u> Use your cartridge pen as a dip pen (but leave the cartridge in place)...

Problem:— No adhesion of ink on surface, run-back and 'beading'.

Solution:— Use a spirit-based calligraphy felt tipped pen.

Problem:— Ink goes on but won't dry.

Solutions:— 1. Sprinkle liberally with fine baby talc, leave for half an hour, and then dust off.
2. Blot gently with blotting paper.
3. Roll a stick of white chalk over the image.

Problem:— Grease or fingerprints on surface.

Solution:— Stop writing, and leave ink to dry on any writing done so far. Sprinkle baby talc over remaining surface and leave for a few minutes. 'Over-write' earlier writing if needed.
(An old fashioned pepper pot filled with baby talc is an ideal companion for this operation).

tricky surfaces

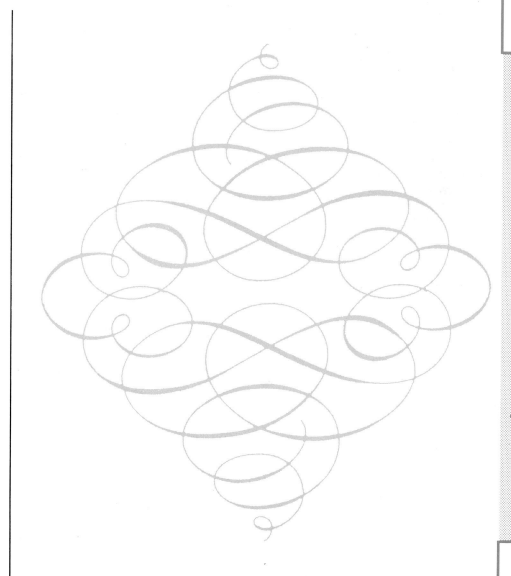

50 calligraphic tips

1 COPYRIGHT — Be very wary of the copyright laws — especially if you intend to reproduce or publish other people's words.

2 SUNSHINE — Do not leave pens, jars and tubes of paint on your desk in the sun.

3 PORTFOLIO — Begin a dated portfolio of your work to show others.

4 CALLIGRAPHIC FILE — Start an index of words or pieces that you would like to do one day.

5 FILLING DIP PENS — Use an ear dropper (available from chemists and very cheap).

6 FIXATIVE — When you're absolutely sure that you've finished the piece and rubbed out your pencil lines, use an art fixative. Do not overspray or the work will look vanished and may 'run'.

7 OPENING STUBBORN JARS & TUBES OF PAINT — Hold under hot water for a few moments, cover with a cloth and open.

8 HUMIDITY — Paper is designed to soak up moisture. Do not leave good papers in a damp or humid place as this will cause 'bleeding' of the ink.

9 STORING PAPER — Where possible, always store paper flat to avoid curl and stretching.

10 CALLIGRAPHIC DRESS — NEVER wear good clothes when writing (for obvious reasons).

11 EYE CARE — When working under a desk lamp for long periods, wear a hat that will shade your eyes—you may look eccentric, but you won't get headaches!

12 VENTILATION — Avoid stuffy rooms. Work outside in the open air if weather permits.

13 TALCUM POWDER — Is perfect for rubbing over a sheet of

paper before you work to remove any grease BUT, ensure that it is completely dusted off so that it will not clog your nib.

14 FLAMMABLE LIQUIDS — Store these in a sensible place; preferably a steel cupboard.

15 LABELS — Always read labels and heed warnings on equipment.

16 SHARP TOOLS — Use an old jam jar and keep to the top of your working area opposite to your writing hand. Tools go in handle first — *always*.

17 BRUSHES — Never, ever lick brushes. Wipe them on soap to maintain point in storage.

18 HANDS — Wash hands both before and after you have been writing.

19 BUSINESS CARD — When confident of your calligraphic efforts, design your own business card.

20 CHARGING FOR YOUR WORK — Establish an hourly rate with a minimum basic charge, *don't work cheaply.*

21 SPELLING — *Always* have your dictionary nearby.

22 CARE OF BRUSHES — Expensive items. Clean in rainwater, but never leave a brush in water for long periods as this will ruin the handle and weaken the spring in the hairs.

23 YOUR OWN ALPHABET — Devise/Design your own calligraphic alphabets early and include in your portfolio of work.

24 PRACTICE PAPER — Old or used computer paper is excellent for both practicing or demonstrating.

25 WATERMARKS — Found on good quality paper of high rag content. When viewed the correct way round, this indicates the right side of the paper to use.

26 CHALK — A stick of chalk makes an ideal calligraphic blotter.

27 FOUNTAIN PENS — Don't travel in an aircraft with a cartridge pen in your pocket — you'll see why!

28 BLEACH WRITING — Using a dip pen, write on a previously inked background with household bleach — it's magic!

29 DRYING INK — On damp days use a hairdryer or desk lamp to dry ink. Don't forget about it whilst drying unless you like curly workpieces.

30 WRITING WITH OTHER FLUIDS — Try red wine. Try food colours.

31 BUYING INK — Always check the cap; if it's gritty, ignore. If the ink is frothy when shaken, ignore it and if it separates, it's old stock, so ignore this as well.

32 METALLIC INKS — Popular for wedding invitations. Must only be used in a dip pen. Shake and stir the ink continuously during use.

33 INK LIFE — No matter how expensive it was, do not keep ink for more than twelve months.

34 DAMP PAPER — Can be dried after a few seconds by placing in a microwave oven.

35 ADHESIVE PLASTIC PUTTY — Blobs of adhesive putty are handy to stop ink bottles sliding down a sloping board.

36 THICKENING INK — Leave the top off the bottle for a few days.

37 ART FIXATIVES — Expensive to buy. Try hair lacquer (test first) *and it smells nice.*

38 THINNING INK — Always use distilled or even rainwater to

thin ink; this will stop it smelling and keep it chemical free. Don't mix inks unless they are the same brand.

39 HAND LOTIONS — Should be avoided as they leave greasy deposits on the paper as your writing hand glides to and fro.

40 LABEL PENS — Most pens look the same. Use adhesive tabs or labels to number the pen and size of nib for easy reference.

41 CLEANING YOUR PEN — Use lukewarm water and a little ammonia. *Never use boiling water.*

42 PEN STORAGE — Always with nibs uppermost.

43 AMMONIA — The calligraphers friend it will clean your pen and loosen ink stains.

44 SMALL CHILDREN — Should be encouraged to watch writing, BUT NEVER THE WRONG WAY ROUND; stand them behind you at your eye level.

45 POSTURE — The more comfortable you are, the better the writing will be on your paper.

46 FLUORESCENT LIGHT — Can really hurt your eyes. Try to avoid long exposure to reflected fluorescent light. Better still, use an incandescent desk lamp.

47 EYEWEAR — People with glasses often can see better when writing if they remove them.

48 RELAXATION — Find some nice music when writing — it really helps.

49 TURNING OFF — Develop *blinkers* when you write; the only thing that matters is that piece of paper in front of you.

50 DATE YOUR WORK — *Always*; this will show you if you are improving or sliding back.

Quills & canepens

Goose, turkey, pelican or even eagle feathers will make good quills. The basic writing cuts are shown. Experiment a little; a quill will either write, or remain a feather.

Balance quill after it has been trimmed.

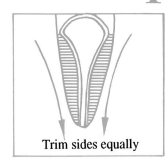

Trim sides equally

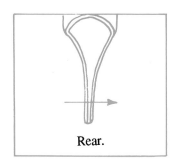

Rear.

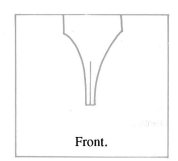

Front.

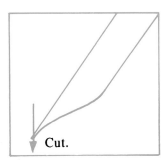

Cut.

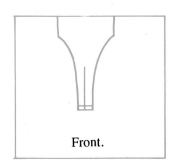

Front.

Gentle pressure will open quill.

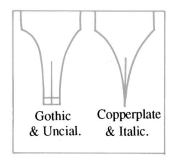

Gothic & Uncial.   Copperplate & Italic.

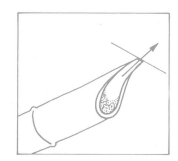

calligraphic fun time

Every budding scribe gets bored. I know that I do. Let's make the pen amaze us by having some calligraphic fun.

if writing words within a circle it is wise to plan them carefully so that a minimum of space is utilized.

Use compass or draw around a saucer...

Writing around a spiral is very tricky but if it works it can look very dynamic. It gets harder?

Turn the work as you go...

from this sample, you can see, don't 'bend' gothic

whereas 'italic' loves to be distorted

AND SO DOES 'UNCIAL' SCRIPT ~ A LOT...

MOTHS

flame

BOOooo

Butterfly

snail

birds

 Love

marching as to war ♪ ♫

 Music

Relax

hooks

 trumpets

 flower

BOUNCE, BOUNCE, AAARH!!

E etc

SEE HOW CREATIVE YOU CAN BE...

alternative alphabets

USING THE SAME BASIC STROKES EXPERIMENT
WITH YOUR LETTERFORMS

A A B C D E E E F F G H I I J J K K
L L M M M N N O O O P P Q Q Q R R
S S S T J T U U V V W W W X Y Y Y Z

YESTERDAY YESTERDAY YESTERDAY

YESTERDAY YESTERDAY

abcdefghijklmnopqr
stuvwxyz

abcdefghijklmnopqr
stuv wxy z

ABCDEFGHIJKLMNOPQR
STUVWXYZ

ᴀ ᴀ A B C Ɔ D E F F G ɦ Ꞥ H I J K
L ᴍ ᴍ ᴍ N N O P P Q R R S T E U ᴠ ᴡ
X ᴠ ᴠ Z

MATThEW ᴍᴀᴛᴛɴᴇᴡ ᴍᴀᴇᴇɴᴇᴡ Matthew

HOW CAN THE SAME WORD LOOK SO
DIFFERENT?

Experiment with the three scripts and
flourishing — be creative!

Lindisfarne   Lindisfarne   Lindisfarne

Lindisfarne   Lindisfarne

Siegfreid   Siegfreid   Siegfreid

---

eire   eire   eire

Intermezzo Andante Largo Pianissimo

TODAY IS THE
TOMORROW
YOU WORRIED
ABOUT
YESTERDAY

Stuck for words? See what you can interpret
using your calligraphic talents.

A BAG OF TOOLS

Isn't it strange
That Princes & Kings,
And Clowns that caper
In sawdust rings,
And Common people
Like you & me
Are builders for Eternity.

Each is given a bag of tools
A shapeless mass,
A book of rules,
And each must make
Ere life is flown—
A stumbling block
Or a stepping stone.

More words _and_ a heading...

framing

If framing your mini-masterpiece it would help to have already bought the frame and that way you can balance your work to suit it.

Where possible have your work professionally framed. A coloured mat will draw the eye to the focal point.

A good frame will not smother or overpower the workpiece.

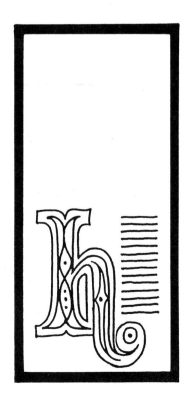

grid sheets

Use a grid sheet under semi-opaque paper such as bank or photocopying paper. The lines should be *just* visible. Ensure the grid sheets do not move during your writing. The individual sheets may be detatched from the work book if this is easier for you.

You may at a later stage wish to rule up your own master sheets to suit your size and weight of script.

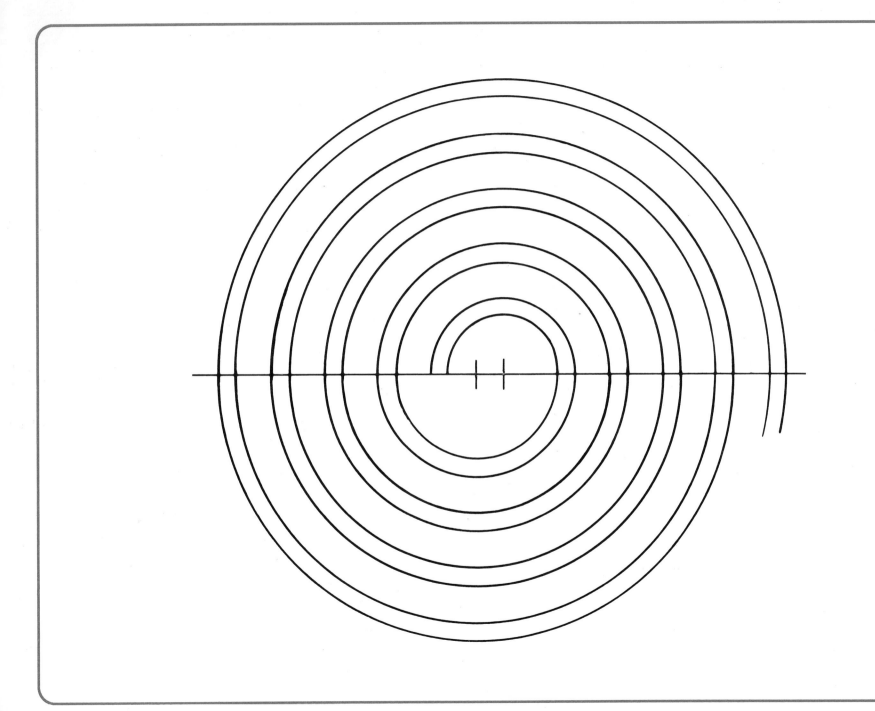

Grid Sheets

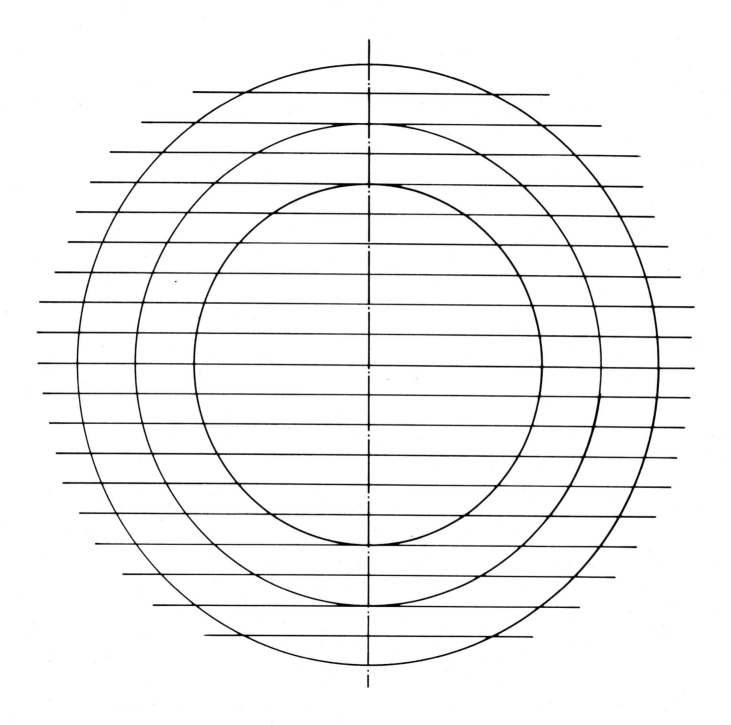

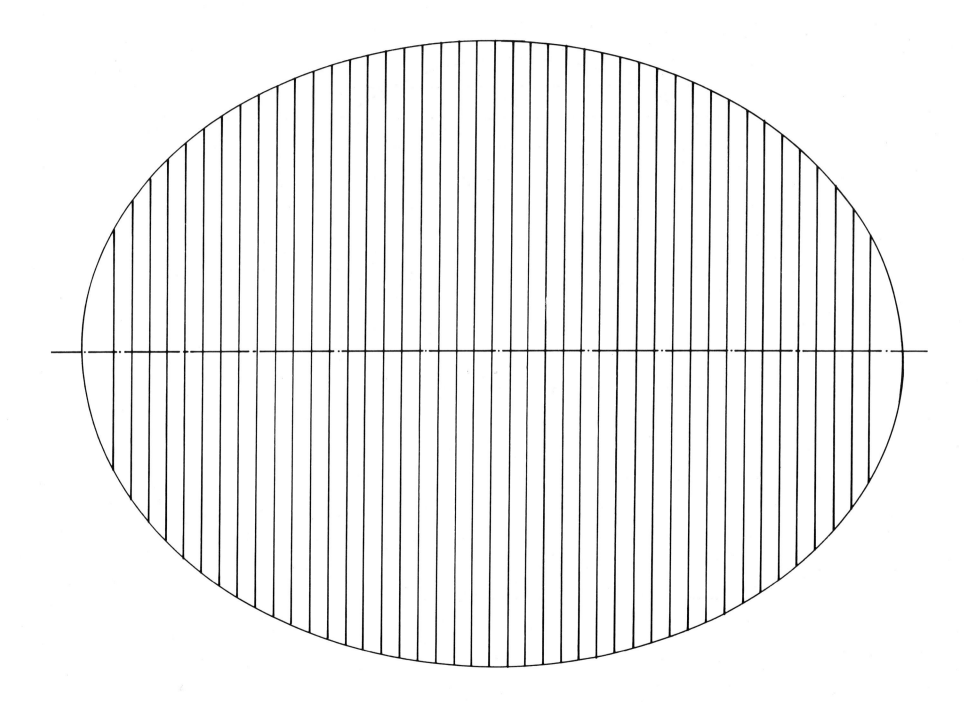

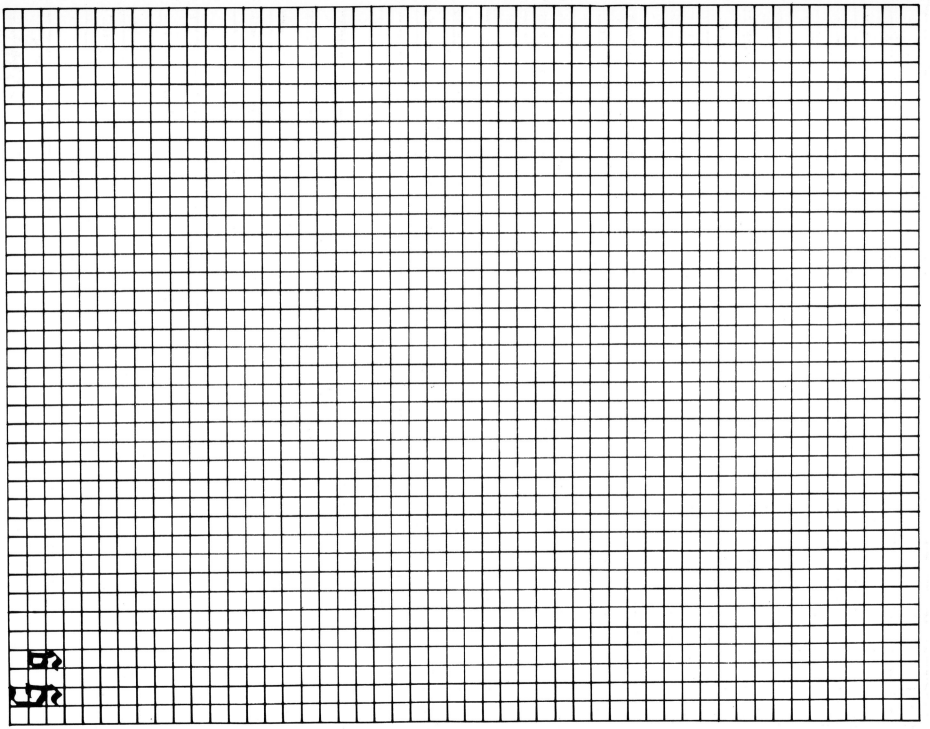

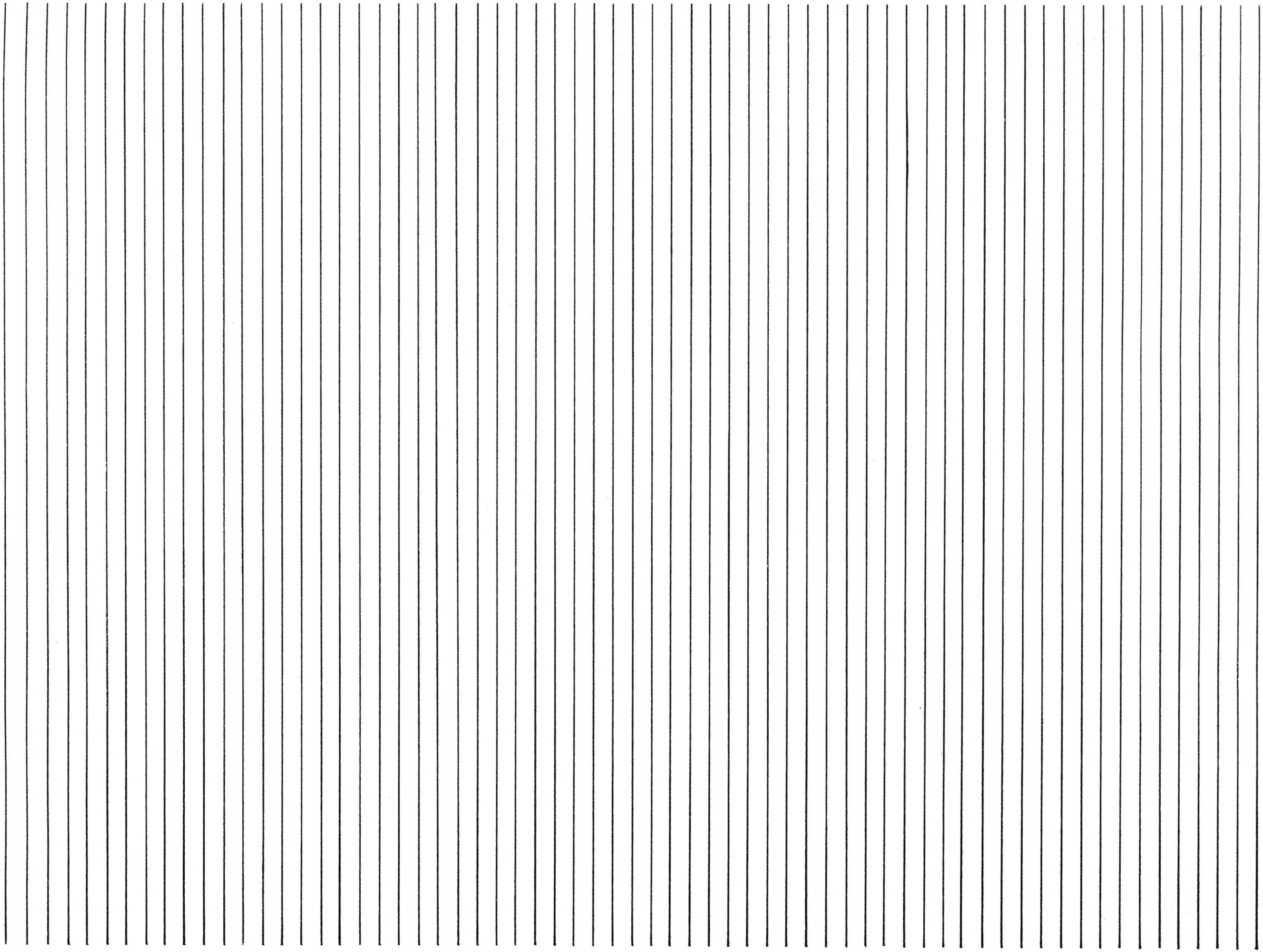

PRACTICE

FIND YOUR WRITING 'ANGLE'

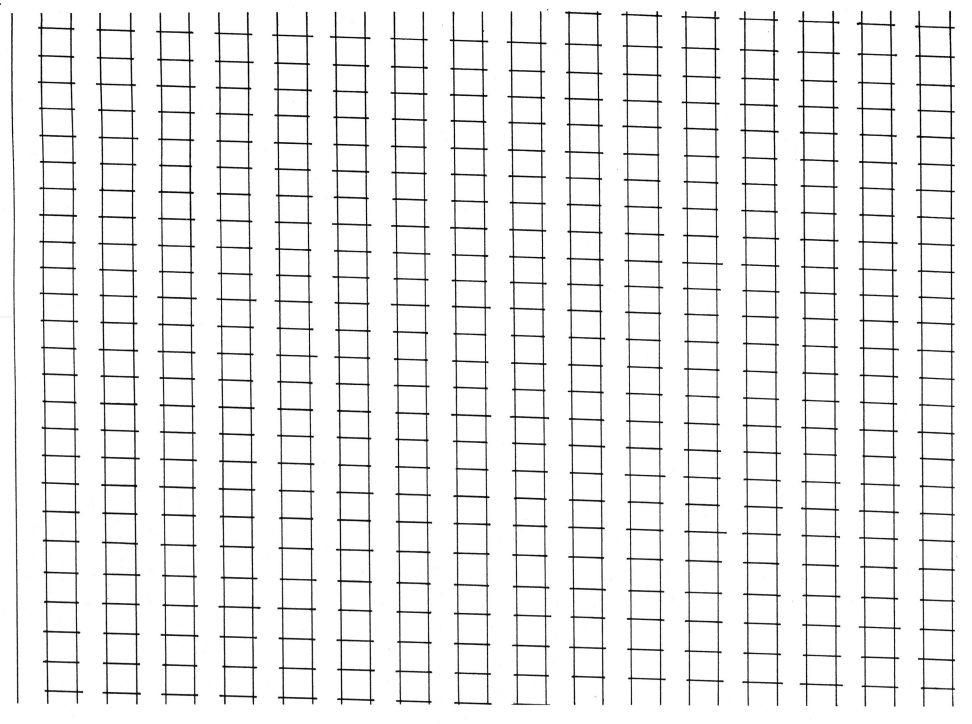

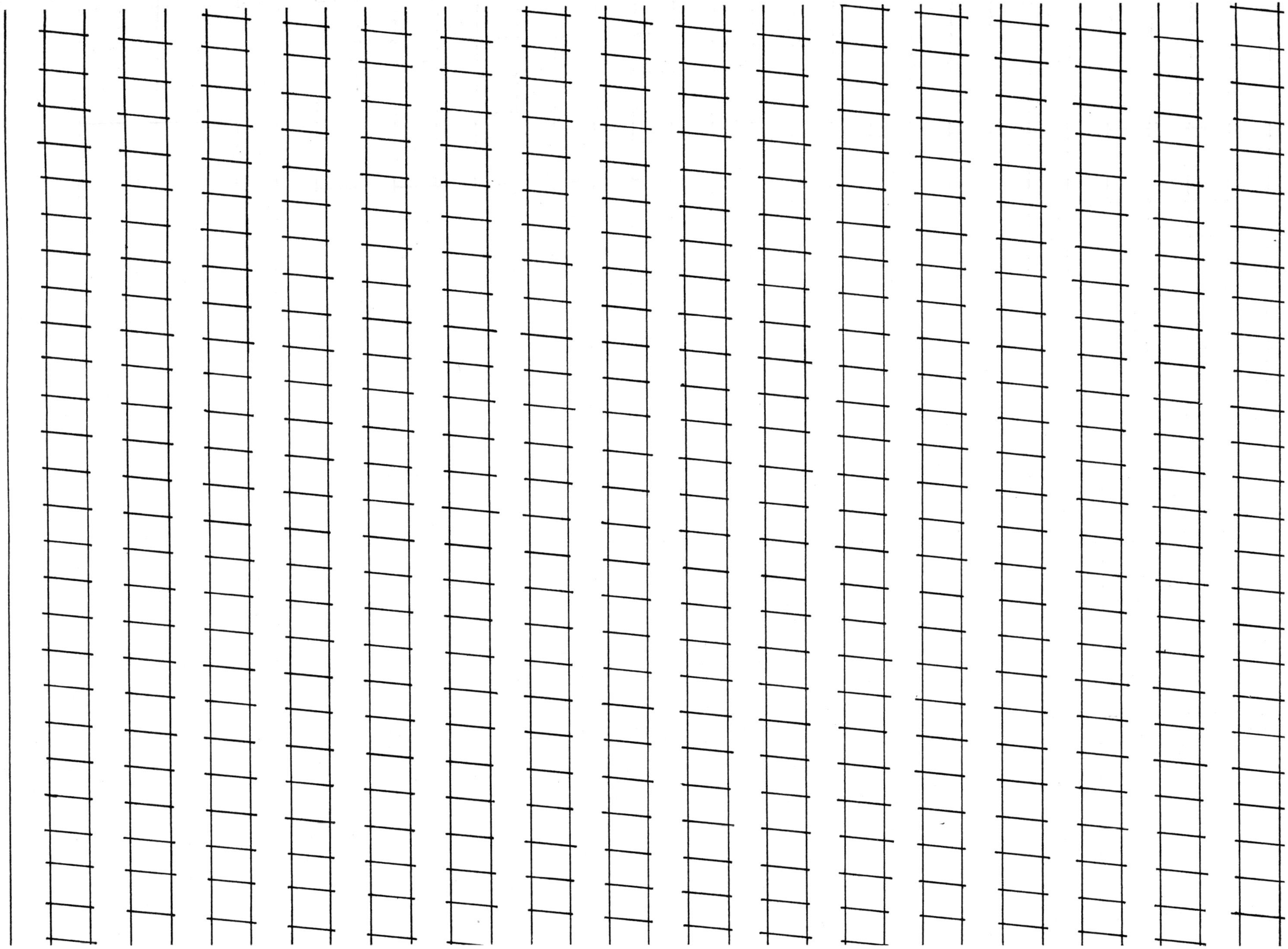

'I suppose that writing is just bending lines nicely'

A nine year old student in a recent calligraphy class

'Good writing should be a harmonic symphony of words'

Jim Billingsley

DON'T DESPAIR IF IT'S NOT GOING TOO WELL...

1. Be <u>comfortable</u> and at <u>peace</u> when you are writing.
2. Write something that you <u>want</u> to write.
3. Ensure that you have a box of <u>tissues</u> nearby — just in case.
4. Find some pleasant and relaxing music.
5. <u>Don't dash</u> into it. Try to pre-plan each line and check the depth of the line spacing between lines.
6. If the telephone rings, <u>let it</u> until you can answer.
7. You might not be doing your <u>best</u> Calligraphy <u>today</u>. Tomorrow it will be better.
8. Spelling may suffer at first.